Mastering

A Step-by-Step Guide to Unlocking Your Psychokinetic Abilities

by Sergio Rijo

SERGIO RIJO

MASTERING TELEKINESIS

A STEP-BY-STEP GUIDE TO DEVELOPING YOUR PSYCHOKINETIC ABILITIES

While every precaution has been taken in the preparation of this book, the publisher assumes no responsibility for errors or omissions, or for damages resulting from the use of the information contained herein.

MASTERING TELEKINESIS: A STEP-BY-STEP GUIDE TO DEVELOPING YOUR PSYCHOKINETIC ABILITIES

First edition. April 17, 2023.

ISBN: 979-8223335221

Written by SERGIO RIJO.

"Telekinesis is not about moving objects with physical force, but about connecting with the energy that surrounds us and learning to direct it with our thoughts and intentions."

Chapter 1: Introduction

Hey there, friend! Welcome to my book on developing telekinesis. I'm so excited to share with you the incredible power of this amazing ability. My name is Sergio Rijo, and I have been studying telekinesis for many years. Throughout my journey, I have discovered the incredible potential of this skill, and I'm here to share it with you.

Let's start with the basics. Telekinesis, also known as psychokinesis, is the ability to move objects with the power of the mind. It is one of the most fascinating and mysterious abilities that human beings can possess. Telekinesis has been the subject of many books, movies, and TV shows, and it has captured the imaginations of people all over the world.

The history of telekinesis dates back to ancient times. There are stories of people with extraordinary abilities to move objects with their minds in many cultures, such as the yogis of India and the shamans of Native American tribes. However, it wasn't until the 20th century that the study of telekinesis began to gain serious attention from scientists.

Unfortunately, there are many misconceptions about telekinesis that have developed over time. Some people believe that telekinesis is purely fictional, while others think that it is only possible for a select few gifted individuals. However, the truth is that telekinesis is a skill that can be developed with practice and dedication.

One of the benefits of learning telekinesis is that it can help you to develop your mental powers and expand your consciousness. Telekinesis is a form of meditation that can help you to become more focused, centered, and aware. It can also help you to increase your confidence and self-esteem, as you gain control over your mind and your environment.

In this book, I will provide you with a step-by-step guide to developing telekinesis. I will cover everything from mental preparation and energy work to advanced techniques like levitation and interdimensional travel. Whether you are a beginner or an advanced practitioner, there is something for everyone in this book.

So get ready to embark on an exciting journey of self-discovery and exploration. By the end of this book, you will have a solid foundation in the art of telekinesis and the tools you need to continue your practice and take your skills to the next level. Let's get started!

Chapter 2: Preparing for Telekinesis

Welcome to Chapter 2 of "How to Develop Telekinesis," where we will discuss the importance of mental preparation before attempting to develop telekinesis.

Mental preparation is an essential part of any new skill you wish to acquire, and telekinesis is no exception. Without the right mindset, it can be challenging to progress and make meaningful gains in your telekinetic abilities. In this chapter, we will explore some effective mental preparation techniques to help you get ready for your telekinetic journey.

The Importance of Mental Preparation

Before you even begin practicing telekinesis, it is crucial to understand that it is not just about moving objects with your mind. Telekinesis is a complex process that requires the coordination of several mental faculties. These include your focus, your visualization skills, and your ability to feel and manipulate energy.

Mental preparation will help you develop these skills and make them second nature, enabling you to concentrate on moving objects with your mind. By preparing your mind for telekinesis, you will find it easier to focus your thoughts, and your visualization skills will improve. Additionally, you will become more sensitive to the energy around you and be better equipped to control it.

Meditation and Mindfulness

Meditation and mindfulness are excellent techniques to help prepare your mind for telekinesis. Both techniques can help you to develop a deeper understanding of your mind and its workings. They can also help you to stay focused, calm, and centered, even in challenging situations.

Meditation involves focusing your mind on a specific object, thought, or sound to achieve a state of mental clarity and emotional calmness. It is a powerful tool for developing focus and concentration, both of which are essential for telekinesis.

Mindfulness, on the other hand, involves being fully present and aware of your thoughts, feelings, and surroundings. It is an excellent technique for developing your visualization skills and increasing your sensitivity to energy.

Visualization Exercises

Visualization exercises are another essential tool for developing your telekinetic abilities. Visualization is the ability to create detailed mental images in your mind's eye. It is a crucial skill for telekinesis, as it allows you to imagine the object you wish to move and direct your energy towards it.

One effective visualization exercise is to picture a simple object, such as an apple, in your mind's eye. Visualize the apple in as much detail as possible, imagining its texture, color, and shape. Focus your energy on the apple and try to move it with your mind. Don't worry if you can't move the apple at first; this exercise is designed to help you develop your visualization skills.

Mental Focus Techniques

Mental focus techniques are crucial for developing the concentration required for telekinesis. One effective technique is to focus your mind on a single object for an extended period. Choose an object and place it in front of you, then focus your mind on it for as long as possible, ignoring any distractions that come your way.

Another technique is to develop your ability to concentrate on different parts of your body. Starting at your toes, mentally scan your body, focusing on each body part in turn, and try to feel the energy flowing through it. This exercise will help you develop your sensitivity to energy and improve your concentration skills.

Mental preparation is a vital component of developing telekinetic abilities. By developing your focus, visualization skills, and energy manipulation abilities, you will be better equipped to move objects with your mind. Meditation, mindfulness, visualization exercises, and mental focus techniques are all effective tools for developing these skills. With the right mindset and preparation, you can develop your telekinetic abilities and achieve your goals.

Chapter 3: Understanding Energy

Welcome to Chapter 3 of our book on How to Develop Telekinesis. In this chapter, we will explore the concept of energy and its relationship to telekinesis.

Energy is the foundation of the universe. It is the driving force behind all that we see and experience. It is what powers our bodies, fuels our emotions, and creates the world around us. Without energy, there would be no life, no movement, and no change. Understanding energy is key to understanding telekinesis.

What is energy?

Energy is a fundamental concept in physics that describes the capacity of a system to perform work. It can exist in various forms such as thermal energy, electrical energy, kinetic energy, potential energy, and many more. However, in the context of telekinesis, we are primarily concerned with subtle energy or life force energy, also known as prana or chi.

Subtle energy is a type of energy that is not readily measurable by conventional scientific methods. It is believed to be the energy that flows through all living things and is responsible for maintaining the balance of the body, mind, and spirit. It is said to be the energy that animates the physical body and gives it life.

The different types of energy

There are many different types of energy, each with its own unique characteristics and properties. Here are some of the most common types of energy:

Thermal energy: This is the energy that is associated with the temperature of an object. It is what causes objects to heat up or cool down.

Electrical energy: This is the energy that is associated with the movement of electrons. It is what powers our electronic devices.

Kinetic energy: This is the energy that is associated with motion. It is what allows objects to move and travel.

Potential energy: This is the energy that is stored in an object due to its position or configuration. It is what allows objects to do work when they are released.

Chemical energy: This is the energy that is stored in the bonds between atoms and molecules. It is what allows chemical reactions to occur.

How energy relates to telekinesis

In the context of telekinesis, energy is believed to be the force that enables us to move objects with our minds. It is said that by focusing and directing our subtle energy, we can create a field of energy around us that interacts with the energy of the object we wish to move. By manipulating this energy field, we can cause the object to move in the desired direction.

Exercises to feel and manipulate energy

Feeling and manipulating energy is an essential skill for telekinesis. Here are some exercises that can help you develop this skill:

The Energy Ball Exercise

The energy ball exercise is a simple exercise that can help you feel and manipulate energy. To do this exercise, follow these steps:

Sit in a comfortable position with your eyes closed.

Take a few deep breaths and relax your body.

Imagine a ball of energy forming in your hands.

Focus your attention on the ball of energy and visualize it getting bigger and brighter.

Move your hands closer together and feel the energy between them.

Slowly move your hands apart and feel the energy ball getting bigger.

Repeat this exercise for a few minutes, focusing on feeling and manipulating the energy ball.

The Energy Scan Exercise

The energy scan exercise is another exercise that can help you feel and manipulate energy. To do this exercise, follow these steps:

Sit in a comfortable position with your eyes closed.

Take a few deep breaths and relax your body.

Imagine a beam of energy coming down from the top of your head and flowing through your body.

Focus your attention on different parts of your body and feel the energy flowing through them.

Visualize the energy flowing through your body like a river, cleansing and purifying your entire being.

When you come across an area where you feel tension or discomfort, visualize the energy flow becoming stronger in that area, helping to release any blockages or negativity.

Repeat this exercise for a few minutes, focusing on feeling and manipulating the energy flowing through your body.

Understanding energy is a crucial step in developing telekinesis. By learning to feel and manipulate subtle energy, you can begin to harness the power of your mind to move objects and influence the world around you. Through exercises like the energy ball and energy scan, you can develop your ability to sense and control this energy. Remember, energy is the foundation of the universe, and by learning to work with it, you can tap into your true potential as a telekinetic.

Chapter 4: Strengthening Your Energy

In this chapter, we will discuss how to strengthen your energy in order to improve your telekinetic abilities.

Techniques to Increase Your Energy

In Chapter 3, we discussed how energy is the driving force behind telekinesis. In order to move objects with our minds, we need to have a strong and steady flow of energy. There are several techniques that can help you increase your energy levels and improve your telekinetic abilities.

Breathing Exercises

Breathing exercises are a simple yet effective way to increase your energy levels. By taking deep, slow breaths, you can increase the amount of oxygen in your body, which in turn increases your energy levels. One simple breathing exercise you can try is to inhale for a count of four, hold for a count of four, and exhale for a count of four. Repeat this exercise for a few minutes each day.

Physical Exercise

Physical exercise is another great way to increase your energy levels. Exercise helps to improve blood flow, which in turn increases the amount of oxygen and nutrients that are delivered to your cells. This can help to improve your energy levels and stamina. Some good exercises to try include jogging, swimming, or yoga.

Meditation

Meditation is a powerful tool for increasing your energy levels. By focusing your mind and calming your thoughts, you can increase the flow of energy throughout your body. Regular meditation practice can help to improve your concentration, reduce stress, and increase your overall sense of well-being.

How to Direct Your Energy

Once you have increased your energy levels, the next step is to learn how to direct your energy. Directing your energy is essential for telekinesis, as it allows you to focus your energy on a specific object or task. Here are some tips on how to direct your energy:

Visualize

Visualizing is a powerful tool for directing your energy. When you visualize an object, you are essentially creating a mental image of it. This mental image can then be used to direct your energy towards that object. To visualize an object, simply close your eyes and imagine it in as much detail as possible.

Focus

Focusing is another important tool for directing your energy. When you focus on an object, you are essentially directing your energy towards it. To focus on an object, simply look at it and concentrate your attention on it.

Intent

Intent is perhaps the most important tool for directing your energy. Intent is your conscious desire to achieve a particular outcome. When you have a clear intent, your energy is automatically directed towards that goal. To use intent for telekinesis, simply focus your mind on the object you wish to move and visualize it moving in the direction you desire.

Building Energy Reserves

In addition to increasing your energy levels and learning how to direct your energy, it is also important to build up your energy reserves. Energy reserves are essentially your body's backup energy supply, which can be used in times of need. Here are some tips on how to build up your energy reserves:

Rest

Rest is essential for building up your energy reserves. When you rest, your body is able to recover and recharge, which can help to increase your energy levels. Make sure to get plenty of sleep each night and take breaks throughout the day.

Nutrition

Nutrition is another important factor in building up your energy reserves. Make sure to eat a healthy, balanced diet that includes plenty of fruits, vegetables, and lean protein. Avoid foods that are high in sugar and processed ingredients, as these can cause energy crashes.

Hydration

Hydration is essential for maintaining your energy levels. Make sure to drink plenty of water throughout the day, as dehydration can cause fatigue and drain your energy reserves.

Stress Management

Stress can drain your energy reserves, so it is important to manage your stress levels. Some effective stress management techniques include meditation, yoga, and deep breathing exercises. It is also important to take breaks throughout the day and avoid overworking yourself.

Understanding Your Energy Limits

While it is important to strengthen your energy and build up your energy reserves, it is also important to understand your energy limits. Pushing yourself too hard can actually have the opposite effect and drain your energy levels. Here are some tips on how to understand your energy limits:

Listen to Your Body

Your body will tell you when it has reached its limit. Pay attention to how you feel and make sure to take breaks when you start to feel fatigued. Pushing yourself too hard can lead to burnout and decreased energy levels.

Set Realistic Goals

Setting realistic goals is essential for understanding your energy limits. If you set goals that are too high, you may end up pushing yourself too hard and draining your energy reserves. Start with small goals and gradually work your way up to more challenging ones.

Take Breaks

Taking breaks throughout the day is essential for maintaining your energy levels. Make sure to take short breaks every hour or two to stretch, rest your eyes, and recharge your energy.

Developing telekinetic abilities requires a strong and steady flow of energy. By increasing your energy levels, learning how to direct your energy, building up your energy reserves, and understanding your energy limits, you can improve your telekinetic abilities and achieve your goals. Remember to take care of yourself and listen to your body, as this will help you maintain your energy levels and prevent burnout. With dedication and practice, you can develop your telekinetic abilities and unlock your full potential.

Chapter 5: Developing Your Senses

In this chapter, we will discuss the importance of developing your senses in order to improve your telekinetic abilities.

The Importance of Senses in Telekinesis

In order to move objects with our minds, we need to be able to sense them. Our senses play a crucial role in telekinesis, as they allow us to perceive and interact with the physical world. By developing our senses, we can improve our ability to sense and interact with objects, which in turn can improve our telekinetic abilities.

Exercises to Develop Your Senses

There are several exercises you can do to develop your senses and improve your telekinetic abilities. Here are some exercises you can try:

Sight

One way to develop your sight is to practice visualization exercises. To do this, simply close your eyes and visualize an object in your mind. Try to visualize it in as much detail as possible, including its shape, color, and texture. With practice, you can improve your ability to visualize objects and enhance your telekinetic abilities.

Hearing

To develop your hearing, try to focus on the sounds around you. Close your eyes and listen to the sounds of nature, such as the rustling of leaves or the chirping of birds. You can also try to listen to music and focus on the different instruments and sounds.

Touch

To develop your sense of touch, try to focus on the sensations in your body. Pay attention to the feeling of the ground beneath your feet, the wind on your skin, or the texture of objects around you. You can also try to touch different objects and focus on the sensations in your fingertips.

Smell

To develop your sense of smell, try to focus on the different scents around you. Take deep breaths and try to identify different smells, such as the smell of flowers or food. You can also try to focus on the smells in different environments, such as the smell of the ocean or a forest.

Taste

To develop your sense of taste, try to focus on the flavors of different foods. Take small bites and focus on the different tastes and textures. You can also try to identify different flavors and ingredients in foods.

How to Apply Your Senses to Telekinesis

Once you have developed your senses, the next step is to learn how to apply them to telekinesis. Here are some tips on how to apply your senses to telekinesis:

Sight

Use your sight to visualize the object you want to move. Close your eyes and imagine the object moving in the direction you desire. With practice, you can improve your ability to visualize objects and move them with your mind.

Hearing

Use your hearing to listen for any subtle changes in the environment around you. Pay attention to any sounds that may indicate movement or energy shifts. This can help you to anticipate and direct the movement of objects.

Touch

Use your sense of touch to feel the energy around you. Place your hands near the object you want to move and focus on the sensations in your fingertips. With practice, you can learn to sense and manipulate energy with your hands.

Smell

Use your sense of smell to identify any subtle changes in the environment around you. Pay attention to any changes in the scent of the air, as this may indicate changes in energy levels or movement.

Taste

Use your sense of taste to identify any subtle changes in the energy around you. Focus on the taste of the air and the energy in the environment. This can help you to sense and manipulate energy with your mind.

Sensory Integration

Sensory integration is the ability to combine and interpret information from different senses. By developing our sensory integration, we can improve our overall ability to sense and interact with the world around us, which can in turn improve our telekinetic abilities. Here are some exercises you can do to develop your sensory integration:

Cross-modal exercises

Cross-modal exercises involve combining information from different senses. For example, you can try to match the sounds of different instruments with their visual appearance or try to match the taste of different foods with their texture. With practice, you can improve your ability to integrate information from different senses and enhance your telekinetic abilities.

Meditation

Meditation is a powerful tool for developing sensory integration. By focusing on your breath and quieting your mind, you can improve your ability to integrate information from different senses. Meditation can also help you to develop a deeper sense of awareness and connection with the world around you.

Yoga

Yoga is another powerful tool for developing sensory integration. By combining physical postures with breathing exercises, yoga can help you to develop a deeper sense of awareness and connection with your body. This can improve your ability to sense and manipulate energy with your mind.

Developing your senses is a crucial step in improving your telekinetic abilities. By practicing exercises to develop your senses, learning to apply your senses to telekinesis, and developing your sensory integration, you can enhance your ability to sense and interact with the world around you. With practice and dedication, you can become a powerful telekinetic and unlock the full potential of your mind.

Chapter 6: Telekinetic Exercises for Beginners

In this chapter, we will discuss some basic telekinetic exercises for beginners. These exercises are designed to help you develop your telekinetic abilities, and to help you gain confidence in your ability to move objects with your mind.

Introduction to Basic Exercises

Before we begin with the exercises, it is important to understand that telekinesis takes practice and patience. You may not see immediate results, but with persistence and dedication, you can improve your abilities over time.

It is also important to have a positive and open mindset. Telekinesis is a mental practice, and your thoughts and emotions can affect your ability to move objects. Believe in yourself and your abilities, and remain open to the possibilities of what you can achieve.

Now, let's get started with some basic exercises.

Moving Small Objects

The first exercise we will discuss is moving small objects. This is a great exercise for beginners, as it allows you to practice telekinesis without having to move large or heavy objects.

To begin, find a small object, such as a paper clip or a piece of paper. Place the object in front of you on a flat surface, such as a table or desk.

Next, focus your mind on the object. Imagine yourself moving the object with your mind, and visualize the object moving in the direction you desire.

As you focus on the object, try to feel a connection with it. Imagine a cord or a beam of energy connecting you to the object.

With practice, you may begin to see the object move. It may only move slightly at first, but with persistence, you can improve your ability to move the object with your mind.

Rolling a Pencil

The next exercise we will discuss is rolling a pencil. This exercise is similar to moving small objects, but it requires more precision and control.

To begin, place a pencil on a flat surface in front of you. Focus your mind on the pencil, and imagine it rolling in a specific direction.

As you focus on the pencil, try to feel a connection with it. Imagine a cord or a beam of energy connecting you to the pencil.

As you continue to focus on the pencil, you may begin to see it roll in the direction you desire. With practice, you can improve your ability to control the movement of the pencil with your mind.

Spinning a Top

The third exercise we will discuss is spinning a top. This exercise requires more focus and control than the previous exercises, as it involves spinning a small object with precision.

To begin, find a small top and place it on a flat surface in front of you. Focus your mind on the top, and imagine it spinning in a specific direction.

As you focus on the top, try to feel a connection with it. Imagine a cord or a beam of energy connecting you to the top.

With practice, you may begin to see the top spin in the direction you desire. It may take some time to get the hang of it, but with persistence, you can improve your ability to spin the top with your mind.

Moving a Matchstick

The final exercise we will discuss is moving a matchstick. This exercise requires even more precision and control than the previous exercises, as it involves moving a small object with a specific motion.

To begin, find a matchstick and place it on a flat surface in front of you. Focus your mind on the matchstick, and imagine it moving in a specific direction with a specific motion.

As you focus on the matchstick, try to feel a connection with it. Imagine a cord or a beam of energy connecting you to the matchstick.

With practice, you may begin to see the matchstick move in the direction and motion you desire. This exercise may take some time to master, but with dedication and persistence, you can improve your ability to move small objects with your mind.

Tips for Success

Here are some additional tips to help you succeed with telekinetic exercises:

Practice regularly. Telekinesis, like any skill, takes practice and repetition to develop. Try to practice these exercises at least a few times a week to see improvement.

Stay relaxed. Tension in your body can interfere with your ability to focus and concentrate. Take a few deep breaths and try to release any tension in your body before beginning each exercise.

Believe in yourself. A positive mindset can go a long way in developing your telekinetic abilities. Believe in your ability to move objects with your mind, and don't let self-doubt hold you back.

Stay patient. You may not see immediate results, but don't get discouraged. Keep practicing and stay patient with yourself.

Telekinesis is a fascinating ability that can be developed with practice and dedication. These basic exercises are a great starting point for beginners, and can help you develop your telekinetic abilities and gain confidence in your skills.

Remember to stay positive, patient, and persistent in your practice. With time and effort, you can improve your telekinetic abilities and achieve amazing results.

Chapter 7: Telekinetic Exercises for Intermediate Practitioners

In this chapter, we will discuss some more advanced telekinetic exercises for intermediate practitioners. These exercises are designed to help you improve your telekinetic abilities and take your skills to the next level.

Moving Larger Objects

The first exercise we will discuss is moving larger objects. This exercise is more challenging than the previous exercises, as it requires you to move heavier and larger objects.

To begin, find a medium-sized object, such as a book or a small box. Place the object in front of you on a flat surface, such as a table or desk.

Next, focus your mind on the object. Imagine yourself moving the object with your mind, and visualize the object moving in the direction you desire.

As you focus on the object, try to feel a connection with it. Imagine a cord or a beam of energy connecting you to the object.

With practice, you may begin to see the object move. It may only move slightly at first, but with persistence, you can improve your ability to move the object with your mind.

Controlling the Trajectory of Objects

The next exercise we will discuss is controlling the trajectory of objects. This exercise requires you to move an object in a specific direction and control its movement.

To begin, find a small object, such as a ball or a toy car. Place the object in front of you on a flat surface.

Next, focus your mind on the object. Imagine yourself moving the object with your mind, and visualize the object moving in a specific direction and trajectory.

As you focus on the object, try to feel a connection with it. Imagine a cord or a beam of energy connecting you to the object.

With practice, you can improve your ability to control the movement of the object with your mind. Try experimenting with different trajectories and directions, and see how much control you can exert over the object.

Moving Multiple Objects at Once

The third exercise we will discuss is moving multiple objects at once. This exercise requires you to move more than one object at the same time, and can be a great challenge for intermediate practitioners.

To begin, find three or four small objects, such as pencils or paper clips. Place the objects in front of you on a flat surface.

Next, focus your mind on the objects. Imagine yourself moving all of the objects with your mind, and visualize them moving in different directions.

As you focus on the objects, try to feel a connection with each one. Imagine a cord or a beam of energy connecting you to each object.

With practice, you can improve your ability to move multiple objects at the same time. Try experimenting with different arrangements of the objects, and see how much control you can exert over them.

Advanced Object Manipulation

The final exercise we will discuss is advanced object manipulation. This exercise is the most challenging of the exercises we have discussed, as it requires you to manipulate objects in complex and intricate ways.

To begin, find a small object, such as a paper clip or a rubber band. Place the object in front of you on a flat surface.

Next, focus your mind on the object. Imagine yourself manipulating the object with your mind, and visualize the object moving in complex and intricate ways.

As you focus on the object, try to feel a connection with it. Imagine a cord or a beam of energy connecting you to the object.

With practice, you can improve your ability to manipulate objects in complex ways. Try experimenting with different movements and patterns, and see how much control you can exert over the object.

These exercises are designed to help intermediate practitioners improve their telekinetic abilities and take their skills to the next level. Remember to practice regularly and be patient with yourself, as developing telekinetic abilities takes time and dedication.

It is also important to have a positive and open mindset. Believe in yourself and your abilities, and trust that you can achieve great things with telekinesis.

As you progress through these exercises, you may begin to notice improvements in your ability to move and manipulate objects with your mind. Celebrate these achievements, no matter how small they may seem, and use them as motivation to continue practicing and improving your skills.

It is also important to remember that telekinesis is not a magic solution to all of life's problems. It is simply a skill, like any other, that can be developed and honed with practice and dedication. Use your telekinetic abilities for positive purposes and always prioritize your own well-being and the well-being of others.

Finally, if you are struggling with these exercises or have any questions or concerns, do not hesitate to seek guidance from experienced practitioners or seek out resources such as books, online communities, or courses.

Remember, the journey of developing telekinetic abilities is a personal one and can be incredibly rewarding. Keep an open mind, stay dedicated, and enjoy the process of discovering what you are truly capable of.

Chapter 8: Telekinetic Exercises for Advanced Practitioners

In this chapter, we will discuss some of the most challenging telekinetic exercises for advanced practitioners. These exercises are designed to push your telekinetic abilities to their limits and help you reach new heights in your practice.

Moving Heavy Objects

Moving heavy objects is one of the most challenging telekinetic exercises for advanced practitioners. This exercise requires you to move objects that are much heavier than anything you have moved before, and requires a great deal of strength and focus.

To begin, find a heavy object, such as a large rock or a piece of furniture. Place the object in front of you on a flat surface, such as the ground or a table.

Next, focus your mind on the object. Imagine yourself moving the object with your mind, and visualize the object moving in the direction you desire.

As you focus on the object, try to feel a connection with it. Imagine a cord or a beam of energy connecting you to the object.

With practice, you may begin to see the object move. It may only move slightly at first, but with persistence, you can improve your ability to move the object with your mind.

Telekinetically Manipulating Water

Telekinetically manipulating water is another challenging exercise for advanced practitioners. This exercise requires you to control the movement of water using your telekinetic abilities.

To begin, fill a clear glass or bowl with water. Place the glass or bowl in front of you on a flat surface.

Next, focus your mind on the water. Imagine yourself moving the water with your mind, and visualize the water moving in a specific direction or forming specific shapes.

As you focus on the water, try to feel a connection with it. Imagine a cord or a beam of energy connecting you to the water.

With practice, you can improve your ability to manipulate the movement of water using your telekinetic abilities. Try experimenting with different shapes and movements, and see how much control you can exert over the water.

Levitation

Levitation is one of the most advanced telekinetic exercises, and requires a great deal of focus and control. This exercise involves lifting yourself or an object off the ground using only your telekinetic abilities.

To begin, find a light object, such as a feather or a small piece of paper. Place the object in front of you on a flat surface.

Next, focus your mind on the object. Imagine yourself lifting the object off the ground using your telekinetic abilities, and visualize the object floating in the air.

As you focus on the object, try to feel a connection with it. Imagine a cord or a beam of energy connecting you to the object.

With practice, you can improve your ability to levitate objects using your telekinetic abilities. As you become more skilled, you can begin to experiment with lifting heavier objects or even yourself off the ground.

These exercises are designed to challenge advanced practitioners and help them reach new heights in their telekinetic practice. Remember to practice regularly and be patient with yourself, as developing telekinetic abilities takes time and dedication.

It is important to approach these exercises with a positive and open mindset. Believe in yourself and your abilities, and don't be afraid to push yourself to new limits. With practice and dedication, you can achieve great things with your telekinetic abilities.

Chapter 9: Telekinetic Energy Fields

In this chapter, we will explore the concept of telekinetic energy fields. Energy fields are an important aspect of telekinesis, as they play a crucial role in the manifestation of telekinetic abilities. By understanding and manipulating energy fields, practitioners can enhance their telekinetic abilities and achieve greater control over the movement of objects.

Understanding Energy Fields

Before we can begin discussing telekinetic energy fields, it is important to have a basic understanding of what energy fields are. In essence, energy fields are invisible areas of energy that surround objects and living beings. These fields are made up of energy particles, which are constantly vibrating and moving.

Everything in the universe has an energy field, including humans, animals, and even inanimate objects like rocks and trees. Energy fields are also present in the environment, such as in the air and water.

Energy fields are not easily perceptible by the human eye, but some people have a natural ability to sense them. This ability is known as clairvoyance, and it allows individuals to see energy fields as colors and shapes. Even if you do not have clairvoyant abilities, you can still learn to sense energy fields through practice and meditation.

Creating and Manipulating Energy Fields

One of the key aspects of telekinesis is the ability to create and manipulate energy fields. By creating an energy field around an object, a practitioner can exert control over the movement of the object.

To create an energy field, begin by focusing your mind on the object you wish to manipulate. Imagine a field of energy forming around the object, and visualize the energy particles vibrating and moving. As you focus on the energy field, try to feel a connection with it, as if the energy is an extension of your own being.

With practice, you can learn to manipulate the energy field to move the object in different directions. For example, if you wish to move an object to the left, imagine the energy field shifting and moving to the left, and visualize the object following the movement of the energy field.

It is important to note that manipulating energy fields requires a great deal of concentration and focus. If you are new to telekinesis, it is recommended that you start with simpler exercises and gradually work your way up to more complex manipulations.

How Energy Fields Relate to Telekinesis

Energy fields are closely related to telekinesis, as they play a crucial role in the manifestation of telekinetic abilities. The ability to manipulate energy fields is essential to exerting control over the movement of objects.

In addition to manipulating energy fields around objects, telekinetic practitioners can also manipulate their own energy fields. By focusing their energy and intention, practitioners can create a strong and focused energy field around themselves, which can enhance their telekinetic abilities and improve their concentration and focus.

Energy fields are also affected by emotions and thoughts. Negative emotions like anger and fear can create chaotic energy fields, which can interfere with telekinetic abilities. Conversely, positive emotions like love and compassion can create coherent energy fields, which can enhance telekinetic abilities.

In conclusion, energy fields are an important aspect of telekinesis, and the ability to manipulate them is essential to developing telekinetic abilities. By practicing and learning to manipulate energy fields, telekinetic practitioners can improve their abilities and achieve greater control over the movement of objects.

Remember to approach telekinesis with an open and positive mindset, and to be patient and persistent in your practice. With dedication and practice, you can achieve greater control over your telekinetic abilities and unlock your full potential as a telekinetic practitioner.

Chapter 10: Telekinetic Techniques for Healing

Telekinesis is a powerful tool that can be used for much more than just moving objects with the mind. It can also be used for healing, as it has the ability to direct and manipulate energy fields. In this chapter, we will discuss how to use telekinesis for healing, techniques for directing energy to heal, and how to use energy fields for healing.

Using Telekinesis for Healing

Telekinesis can be used for healing in many different ways. It has been used to help alleviate physical pain, emotional distress, and mental health issues. The key to using telekinesis for healing is to focus on directing and manipulating energy fields.

Energy fields are a vital component of the human body. They exist in and around the body, and are responsible for regulating the flow of energy throughout the body. When these energy fields become disrupted or imbalanced, it can lead to physical, emotional, and mental health problems.

Using telekinesis for healing involves directing energy to the areas of the body that need healing. By doing so, you can help to restore balance to the energy fields and promote healing.

Techniques for Directing Energy to Heal

There are several different techniques that can be used to direct energy to heal. These techniques involve visualizing and manipulating energy fields with the mind.

One technique is to visualize energy flowing into the body through the crown of the head. Imagine the energy flowing down through the body, and into the area that needs healing. Visualize the energy flowing into the affected area, and imagine it filling the area with healing energy.

Another technique is to use the hands to direct energy. Place your hands over the affected area, and visualize energy flowing through your hands and into the area that needs healing. You can also use your hands to move energy around the body, directing it to where it is needed most.

A third technique is to use visualization to manipulate energy fields. Visualize the energy field around the affected area, and imagine it becoming brighter and more vibrant. You can also imagine the energy field being repaired or strengthened, helping to restore balance to the area.

How to Use Energy Fields for Healing

In addition to directing energy to heal, you can also use energy fields themselves for healing. Energy fields can be manipulated and directed to help promote healing and balance in the body.

One way to use energy fields for healing is to focus on strengthening the energy field around the body. Visualize the energy field becoming brighter and more vibrant, and imagine it expanding outwards. By doing so, you can help to protect the body from negative energy and promote overall health and well-being.

Another way to use energy fields for healing is to focus on balancing the energy fields within the body. Visualize the energy flowing smoothly throughout the body, and imagine any areas of blockage or disruption being cleared away. By doing so, you can promote balance and harmony within the body, which can help to alleviate a variety of health problems.

Telekinesis can be a powerful tool for healing, as it has the ability to direct and manipulate energy fields. By focusing on directing energy to heal, using techniques for directing energy, and using energy fields themselves for healing, you can help to promote balance and well-being in the body. Remember to approach telekinetic healing with a positive and open mindset, and to always listen to your body and seek professional medical advice when necessary. With practice and dedication, you can use telekinesis for healing and promote overall health and well-being in yourself and others.

Chapter 11: Telekinetic Techniques for Protection

Telekinesis is not just limited to moving objects or manipulating energy fields. It can also be used for protection. In this chapter, we will discuss the various techniques for using telekinesis to create protective energy shields and how to use energy fields for protection.

Using Telekinesis for Protection

The ability to create a protective energy shield using telekinesis is one of the most valuable skills that a practitioner can have. This skill can be used in various situations where one might feel threatened or vulnerable. The protective energy shield is created by manipulating energy fields to form a barrier around the body or the environment, preventing any negative energy or harmful entities from entering.

There are several ways to create a protective energy shield using telekinesis, and we will discuss some of the most effective techniques.

Techniques for Creating Protective Energy Shields

Visualization Technique

The visualization technique is one of the simplest techniques for creating a protective energy shield. To begin, find a quiet and comfortable place where you won't be disturbed. Close your eyes and take a few deep breaths to calm your mind.

Next, visualize a bright white light surrounding your body. Imagine this light expanding and growing until it forms a protective shield around your body. Visualize the shield as a solid barrier that is impenetrable to any negative energy or harmful entities.

As you visualize the shield, focus on the intention of protection. Imagine the shield absorbing any negative energy or harmful entities and transmuting them into positive energy. Hold this visualization for as long as you feel necessary.

Energy Manipulation Technique

The energy manipulation technique involves manipulating the energy fields around your body to create a protective shield. To begin, find a quiet and comfortable place where you won't be disturbed. Close your eyes and take a few deep breaths to calm your mind.

Next, visualize the energy fields around your body. Focus on the intention of protection and imagine the energy fields expanding and growing until they form a protective shield around your body.

As you manipulate the energy fields, imagine them absorbing any negative energy or harmful entities and transmuting them into positive energy. Hold this visualization for as long as you feel necessary.

Object Manipulation Technique

The object manipulation technique involves using telekinesis to manipulate objects to create a protective shield. To begin, find a quiet and comfortable place where you won't be disturbed. Choose an object that you feel connected to, such as a crystal or a piece of jewelry.

Next, focus your mind on the object and visualize it becoming imbued with a protective energy. Imagine the energy spreading from the object and forming a shield around your body.

As you manipulate the object, imagine the shield absorbing any negative energy or harmful entities and transmuting them into positive energy. Hold this visualization for as long as you feel necessary.

How to Use Energy Fields for Protection

Energy fields are an essential aspect of telekinesis and can also be used for protection. By manipulating energy fields, you can create a protective shield around yourself or others.

To use energy fields for protection, follow these steps:

Find a quiet and comfortable place where you won't be disturbed.

Close your eyes and take a few deep breaths to calm your mind.

Visualize the energy fields around your body. Imagine them expanding and growing until they form a protective shield.

Focus on the intention of protection. Imagine the shield absorbing any negative energy or harmful entities and transmuting them into positive energy.

Hold this visualization for as long as you feel necessary.

Energy fields can also be used to protect others. To protect someone else using energy fields, follow these steps:

Find a quiet and comfortable place where you won't be disturbed.

Close your eyes and take a few deep breaths to calm your mind.

Visualize the person you want to protect in front of you.

Focus on the intention of protection. Imagine the energy fields around your body expanding and growing until they form a protective shield around the other person.

As you manipulate the energy fields, imagine them absorbing any negative energy or harmful entities and transmuting them into positive energy.

Hold this visualization for as long as you feel necessary.

Telekinesis is a powerful tool that can be used for many purposes, including protection. By using telekinetic techniques to create protective energy shields, practitioners can protect themselves and others from negative energy and harmful entities. Visualization, energy manipulation, and object manipulation are all effective techniques for creating protective shields. Energy fields can also be manipulated to create protective shields around the body or environment. With practice and dedication, anyone can learn to use telekinesis for protection and create a safer, more positive environment.

Chapter 12: Telekinetic Techniques for Manifestation

Telekinesis is a powerful tool that can be used for many purposes, including manifestation. Manifestation is the process of bringing your desires into reality, and it is a technique that has been used by spiritual practitioners for centuries.

In this chapter, we will explore how telekinesis can be used for manifestation, techniques for visualizing your desires, and how to direct your energy towards manifestation.

Using Telekinesis for Manifestation

Telekinesis can be used for manifestation by directing your energy towards your desires. When you focus your energy on your desires, you can bring them into reality.

To use telekinesis for manifestation, follow these steps:

Visualize your desire: The first step in manifestation is to visualize your desire. Close your eyes and imagine what it would look like if your desire was already manifested. Use all of your senses to imagine the details of your desire, such as the colors, smells, and sounds.

Focus your energy: Once you have visualized your desire, focus your energy on it. Imagine that you are directing your energy towards your desire, and that your energy is helping to bring your desire into reality.

Believe in your manifestation: Finally, it is important to believe that your manifestation is possible. Believe that your desire is already on its way to you, and that your energy is helping to bring it into reality.

Techniques for Visualizing Your Desires

Visualization is a powerful technique that can be used to help manifest your desires. When you visualize your desires, you are using your imagination to create a mental image of what you want to manifest.

Here are some techniques for visualizing your desires:

Create a vision board: A vision board is a collage of images that represent your desires. It is a powerful tool for visualization, as it helps you to focus your energy on your desires.

To create a vision board, gather images that represent your desires and glue them onto a piece of paper or a poster board. Place your vision board in a prominent location where you will see it every day.

Use affirmations: Affirmations are positive statements that help to reprogram your subconscious mind. By repeating affirmations, you can train your mind to focus on your desires.

To use affirmations, choose a statement that represents your desire, such as "I am wealthy" or "I am healthy." Repeat the affirmation to yourself several times a day, and visualize your desire as you do so.

Meditate on your desires: Meditation is a powerful technique for visualization. When you meditate, you are able to quiet your mind and focus your energy on your desires.

To meditate on your desires, find a quiet and comfortable place where you won't be disturbed. Close your eyes and take a few deep breaths to calm your mind. Then, visualize your desire and focus your energy on it. Hold this visualization for as long as you feel necessary.

How to Direct Your Energy Towards Manifestation

Directing your energy towards manifestation is an important aspect of telekinesis. When you direct your energy towards your desires, you are able to bring them into reality.

Here are some techniques for directing your energy towards manifestation:

Use intention: Intention is a powerful tool for directing your energy. When you set an intention, you are focusing your energy on a specific outcome.

To use intention, set a clear intention for what you want to manifest. Focus your energy on your intention, and believe that it is already on its way to you.

Use visualization: Visualization is another powerful tool for directing your energy. When you visualize your desires, you are able to create a mental image of what you want to manifest.

To use visualization, visualize your desire and focus your energy on it. Imagine that your energy is helping to bring your desire into reality.

Practice mindfulness: Mindfulness is the practice of being present in the moment. When you are mindful, you are able to focus your energy on the present moment, and you are less likely to get distracted by negative thoughts or worries.

To practice mindfulness, take a few deep breaths and focus on the present moment. Notice your surroundings, and pay attention to your thoughts and feelings without judgment.

Use positive affirmations: Positive affirmations are powerful tools for directing your energy towards manifestation. When you repeat positive affirmations, you are reprogramming your subconscious mind to focus on your desires.

To use positive affirmations, choose a statement that represents your desire, such as "I am wealthy" or "I am healthy." Repeat the affirmation to yourself several times a day, and visualize your desire as you do so.

Telekinesis can be a powerful tool for manifestation. By directing your energy towards your desires and using visualization and intention, you can bring your desires into reality.

It is important to remember that manifestation is not a quick fix, and it requires patience and persistence. It is also important to believe in yourself and your abilities, and to have faith that your desires are already on their way to you.

By practicing these techniques for telekinetic manifestation, you can tap into the power of your mind and energy, and create the life that you desire.

Chapter 13: Telekinetic Techniques for Mind Reading

Telekinesis is a powerful tool that can be used for many purposes, including mind reading. Mind reading is the ability to read the thoughts and emotions of others, and it is a technique that has been used by spiritual practitioners for centuries.

In this chapter, we will explore how telekinesis can be used for mind reading, techniques for reading thoughts, and how to protect yourself from unwanted telepathic communication.

Using Telekinesis for Mind Reading

Telekinesis can be used for mind reading by tapping into the energy fields of others. By focusing your energy on the energy field of another person, you can gain access to their thoughts and emotions.

To use telekinesis for mind reading, follow these steps:

Focus on the person: The first step in mind reading is to focus on the person whose thoughts you want to read. Focus your energy on their energy field, and imagine that you are connecting with them on a deep level.

Clear your mind: Next, it is important to clear your mind of all distractions. Focus your energy on your breathing, and let go of any thoughts that may be distracting you.

Visualize the person's thoughts: Once your mind is clear, visualize the person's thoughts. Imagine that you are seeing their thoughts as if they were projected onto a movie screen.

Listen to your intuition: Finally, it is important to listen to your intuition. Pay attention to any impressions or feelings that come up, as they may be clues to the person's thoughts.

Techniques for Reading Thoughts

There are many techniques for reading thoughts, and the most effective technique will depend on the individual. Here are some techniques that may be helpful:

Empathy: Empathy is the ability to feel the emotions of others. By tapping into the emotions of another person, you may be able to gain insight into their thoughts.

To use empathy, focus on the person's emotions. Imagine that you are feeling their emotions as if they were your own. Pay attention to any thoughts that come up as you do so.

Telepathy: Telepathy is the ability to communicate with others through thoughts. By tapping into the thoughts of another person, you may be able to gain insight into their thoughts.

To use telepathy, focus on the person's thoughts. Imagine that you are communicating with them through thoughts. Pay attention to any thoughts that come up as you do so.

Intuition: Intuition is the ability to sense information without the use of the five senses. By tapping into your intuition, you may be able to gain insight into the thoughts of others.

To use intuition, focus on the person and pay attention to any impressions or feelings that come up. Trust your intuition, even if it doesn't make sense at first.

How to Protect Yourself from Unwanted Telepathic Communication

While telepathic communication can be a powerful tool, it is important to protect yourself from unwanted telepathic communication. Here are some techniques for protecting yourself:

Set boundaries: Set clear boundaries for yourself and others. Let others know that you do not want to receive telepathic communication unless you have given them permission to do so.

Visualize a shield: Visualize a shield of white light surrounding you. Imagine that this shield is protecting you from unwanted telepathic communication.

Use affirmations: Use affirmations to protect yourself from unwanted telepathic communication. Repeat affirmations such as "I am protected from unwanted telepathic communication" or "I am in control of my telepathic abilities."

Use grounding techniques: Grounding techniques can help you to stay centered and focused. To ground yourself, imagine that you are connected to the earth. Imagine that roots are growing from your feet and into the earth, grounding you in the present moment.

Telekinesis can be a powerful tool for mind reading, but it is important to use it with caution and respect for others' privacy. Mind reading can be a useful tool for gaining insight into the thoughts and emotions of others, but it should never be used to manipulate or harm others.

If you are interested in developing your telekinetic abilities for mind reading, it is important to practice regularly and seek guidance from experienced practitioners. It may also be helpful to work on developing your intuition and empathy, as these skills can be beneficial for mind reading.

Remember, telepathic communication is a two-way street, and it is important to respect the boundaries and consent of others. Always ask for permission before attempting to read someone's thoughts, and be mindful of the impact your telepathic communication may have on others.

Telekinesis can be a powerful tool for mind reading, but it should be used with caution and respect for others. By following these techniques and protection methods, you can develop your telekinetic abilities for mind reading while maintaining healthy boundaries and respect for others.

Chapter 14: Telekinetic Techniques for Teleportation

Teleportation has long been a staple of science fiction, but with the power of telekinesis, it may be possible to bring this technology to reality. In this chapter, we will explore how telekinesis can be used for teleportation, techniques for moving objects through space, and the potential of teleportation in the future.

Using Telekinesis for Teleportation

Teleportation is the ability to move an object or person from one location to another instantly. While this may seem like an impossible feat, it may be possible with the power of telekinesis.

To use telekinesis for teleportation, follow these steps:

Focus on the object: The first step in teleportation is to focus on the object that you want to move. Focus your energy on the object, and imagine that you are connecting with it on a deep level.

Visualize the destination: Next, it is important to visualize the destination. Imagine the object appearing in the new location, and focus your energy on that location.

Move the object: Finally, use your telekinetic powers to move the object to the new location. Imagine the object disappearing from its current location and reappearing in the new location.

It is important to note that teleportation is an advanced telekinetic technique, and it may take time and practice to master.

Techniques for Moving Objects through Space

While teleportation may be the ultimate goal, there are many techniques for moving objects through space that can be practiced first. Here are some techniques that may be helpful:

Push and pull: The most basic telekinetic technique is to push and pull objects with your mind. Start by focusing on a small object, such as a pencil or pen. Focus your energy on the object, and imagine that you are pushing or pulling it with your mind.

Levitation: Once you have mastered the push and pull technique, you can move on to levitation. Focus your energy on the object, and imagine that you are lifting it with your mind. Start with a small object, such as a feather, and work your way up to larger objects.

Transportation: Transportation is the ability to move an object from one location to another without physically touching it. To practice transportation, focus your energy on the object, and imagine that you are moving it through space to a new location.

The Potential of Teleportation in the Future

While teleportation may seem like something out of a science fiction novel, it has the potential to revolutionize the way we travel and move objects. Here are some potential uses for teleportation in the future:

Transportation: Teleportation could be used for transportation, allowing people to travel from one location to another instantly. This could revolutionize the airline industry and make travel faster and more efficient.

Emergency response: Teleportation could also be used in emergency response situations, allowing emergency personnel to instantly transport themselves and equipment to the scene of an emergency.

Space exploration: Teleportation could be used for space exploration, allowing astronauts to instantly transport themselves and equipment to different locations in space.

Logistics: Teleportation could also be used for logistics, allowing goods to be transported instantly from one location to another.

While these applications may seem far-fetched, the potential of teleportation is vast, and with continued research and development, it may become a reality in the future.

Teleportation may seem like a far-off dream, but with the power of telekinesis, it may be possible to bring this technology to reality. By focusing your energy on objects and visualizing their movement through space, you can begin to practice the techniques necessary for teleportation. Whether it is used for transportation, emergency response, space exploration, or logistics, teleportation has the potential to revolutionize the way we move objects and travel.

Chapter 15: Telekinetic Techniques for Time Travel

Time travel is a concept that has fascinated people for centuries. It is the idea that we can travel back and forth in time, visiting different eras and experiencing events that have already happened or that will happen in the future. While time travel may seem like science fiction, some believe that it is possible through the use of telekinesis.

In this chapter, we will explore how telekinesis can be used for time travel, techniques for manipulating time, and the ethics of time travel.

Using Telekinesis for Time Travel

Telekinesis can be used for time travel by manipulating the energy fields that surround us. By tapping into these energy fields, we can move through time and space, visiting different eras and experiencing different events.

To use telekinesis for time travel, follow these steps:

Focus on the destination: The first step in time travel is to focus on the destination. Decide where and when you want to go, and visualize yourself being there.

Connect with the energy field: Once you have a clear image of your destination in your mind, focus your energy on the energy field that surrounds you. Imagine that you are connecting with the energy field, and that it is guiding you to your destination.

Move through time: As you connect with the energy field, imagine that you are moving through time. Visualize yourself moving backwards or forwards in time, until you reach your destination.

Techniques for Manipulating Time

There are many techniques for manipulating time, and the most effective technique will depend on the individual. Here are some techniques that may be helpful:

Visualization: Visualization is the ability to create images in your mind. By visualizing yourself in a different time or place, you may be able to manipulate time and travel through it.

To use visualization, focus on the destination you want to travel to. Imagine yourself being there, and focus your energy on the energy field that surrounds you.

Meditation: Meditation is a technique that can help you to focus your energy and connect with the energy fields that surround you. By meditating regularly, you may be able to develop your telekinetic abilities and manipulate time more effectively.

To use meditation, find a quiet place where you can sit comfortably. Focus your energy on your breathing, and let go of any thoughts that may be distracting you. Visualize yourself connecting with the energy field, and imagine that it is guiding you through time.

Telekinesis: Telekinesis is the ability to move objects through space using the power of the mind. By using telekinesis, you may be able to manipulate time and move through it.

To use telekinesis, focus your energy on the object you want to move. Imagine that you are moving the object through time and space, and focus your energy on the energy field that surrounds you.

The Ethics of Time Travel

While time travel may seem like an exciting and adventurous concept, it raises many ethical questions. For example, is it ethical to travel back in time and change events that have already happened? What are the consequences of altering the course of history?

There is no easy answer to these questions, as the ethics of time travel are a complex and controversial topic. Some argue that time travel should be used for scientific research and exploration, while others argue that it should be used for personal gain or entertainment.

Ultimately, the ethics of time travel will depend on the individual and their intentions. If time travel is used for the greater good, it may be seen as ethical. However, if it is used for personal gain or to harm others, it may be seen as unethical.

Telekinesis is a powerful tool that can be used for many purposes, including time travel. While time travel may seem like science fiction, some believe that it is possible through the use of telekinesis.

If you are interested in exploring the possibilities of time travel through telekinesis, it is important to approach it with caution and respect for the ethics involved. Remember that altering the course of history could have unforeseen consequences and impact the lives of many people. It is important to consider the potential consequences before engaging in time travel.

Furthermore, it is important to note that the concept of time travel through telekinesis is still highly debated in the scientific community. While there have been anecdotal accounts of individuals claiming to have experienced time travel, there is no empirical evidence to support the idea. As such, it is important to approach this topic with an open mind and a healthy dose of skepticism.

Overall, the concept of time travel through telekinesis is an intriguing one that is sure to capture the imagination of many. Whether or not it is possible remains to be seen, but the potential implications are certainly worth exploring. By delving into the techniques and ethics involved, we can gain a deeper understanding of this fascinating topic and its implications for our understanding of the universe.

Chapter 16: Telekinetic Techniques for Astral Projection

Have you ever wanted to explore different realms beyond our physical world? Or maybe you've experienced lucid dreaming and wonder if there's a way to intentionally leave your body and explore new dimensions. If so, astral projection may be the practice for you. In this chapter, we will explore how telekinesis can be used for astral projection, techniques for leaving your physical body, and how to explore the astral realm.

Using Telekinesis for Astral Projection

Telekinesis can be used for astral projection by tapping into the energy fields that surround us. By connecting with these fields, we can release our astral body from our physical body and explore new dimensions. Here's how to use telekinesis for astral projection:

Prepare for meditation: Before attempting astral projection, it's important to prepare your mind and body. Set aside some time in a quiet and comfortable space where you can meditate without interruptions.

Connect with your energy field: Focus your attention on the energy field that surrounds your body. Imagine that you are connecting with this field, and that it is guiding you towards your astral body.

Release your astral body: Visualize your astral body lifting out of your physical body, slowly and gently. Imagine that you are using your telekinetic abilities to move your astral body through the energy field that surrounds you.

Techniques for Leaving Your Physical Body

Leaving your physical body can be challenging, especially if you've never done it before. Here are some techniques that may be helpful:

Meditation: Meditation is a powerful tool that can help you to relax your body and focus your mind. By meditating regularly, you can develop the ability to release your astral body from your physical body.

Deep breathing: Deep breathing is another effective technique for preparing your body and mind for astral projection. Take slow, deep breaths and focus your attention on your breath. As you exhale, imagine that you are releasing your astral body from your physical body.

Relaxation techniques: There are many relaxation techniques that can help you to release tension and stress from your body. Try progressive muscle relaxation, where you tense and release different muscle groups, or take a warm bath or shower before your meditation.

How to Explore the Astral Realm

Once you've released your astral body from your physical body, you can explore the astral realm. Here are some tips for exploring this new dimension:

Set an intention: Before you leave your body, set an intention for your journey. Decide what you want to explore or learn, and focus your attention on this intention as you travel through the astral realm.

Stay aware: As you explore the astral realm, stay aware of your surroundings. Observe any sights, sounds, or sensations you experience, and try to stay present in the moment.

Interact with your surroundings: You can interact with the astral realm in many ways. Try talking to beings you encounter, or explore new environments by flying or swimming through them.

Return to your physical body: When you are ready to return to your physical body, focus your attention on it and imagine yourself re-entering it. Gently move your fingers and toes, and slowly open your eyes.

Astral projection is a powerful practice that can help us explore new dimensions beyond our physical world. By using telekinesis, we can release our astral body from our physical body and explore the astral realm. With regular practice and dedication, anyone can learn to astral project and expand their consciousness. Just remember to always approach this practice with respect and intention, and be patient with yourself as you learn and grow.

Chapter 17: Telekinetic Techniques for Interdimensional Travel

Telekinesis is a powerful tool that can be used for many purposes, including interdimensional travel. The concept of traveling between different dimensions has been explored in science fiction and fantasy for decades, but some believe that it is possible through the use of telekinesis.

In this chapter, we will explore how telekinesis can be used for interdimensional travel, techniques for accessing other dimensions, and the potential dangers of interdimensional travel.

Using Telekinesis for Interdimensional Travel

Telekinesis can be used for interdimensional travel by manipulating the energy fields that exist between different dimensions. By tapping into these energy fields, we can move between dimensions and explore new realities.

To use telekinesis for interdimensional travel, follow these steps:

Focus on the destination: The first step in interdimensional travel is to focus on the destination. Decide where you want to go, and visualize yourself being there.

Connect with the energy field: Once you have a clear image of your destination in your mind, focus your energy on the energy field that exists between dimensions. Imagine that you are connecting with the energy field, and that it is guiding you to your destination.

Move between dimensions: As you connect with the energy field, imagine that you are moving between dimensions. Visualize yourself passing through a portal or doorway, and entering a new reality.

Techniques for Accessing Other Dimensions

There are many techniques for accessing other dimensions, and the most effective technique will depend on the individual. Here are some techniques that may be helpful:

Meditation: Meditation is a powerful tool that can help you to focus your energy and connect with the energy fields that exist between dimensions. By meditating regularly, you may be able to develop your telekinetic abilities and access other dimensions more effectively.

To use meditation, find a quiet place where you can sit comfortably. Focus your energy on your breathing, and let go of any thoughts that may be distracting you. Visualize yourself connecting with the energy field between dimensions, and imagine that it is guiding you to your destination.

Visualization: Visualization is the ability to create images in your mind. By visualizing yourself in another dimension, you may be able to access it and explore it.

To use visualization, focus on the dimension you want to explore. Imagine yourself being there, and focus your energy on the energy field that exists between dimensions.

Lucid dreaming: Lucid dreaming is the ability to be aware that you are dreaming, and to control your dreams. By practicing lucid dreaming, you may be able to access other dimensions while you sleep.

To use lucid dreaming, focus on the dimension you want to explore before you go to sleep. Imagine yourself being there, and visualize yourself entering the dimension as you fall asleep.

The Potential Dangers of Interdimensional Travel

While interdimensional travel may seem like an exciting and adventurous concept, it can also be dangerous. Traveling between dimensions can expose us to new realities that we may not be prepared for, and can lead to physical and emotional harm.

Some potential dangers of interdimensional travel include:

Physical harm: Traveling between dimensions can expose us to new physical laws and environments that may harm us. For example, traveling to a dimension with different gravity or atmosphere could be dangerous to our health.

Mental harm: Exploring new realities can be overwhelming and emotionally taxing, and can lead to mental health issues such as anxiety and depression.

Exposure to new entities: Interdimensional travel can expose us to new entities and beings that we may not be prepared for. Some of these beings may be hostile or dangerous.

Loss of identity: Traveling between dimensions can lead to a loss of identity as we are exposed to new cultures, beliefs, and ways of life. This can be a disorienting and unsettling experience.

It is important to approach interdimensional travel with caution and to be prepared for the potential dangers. Before attempting interdimensional travel, consider the following:

Research: Do your research on the dimension you want to explore. Learn as much as you can about its physical laws, environment, and entities. This will help you to be prepared for what you may encounter.

Mental and emotional preparation: Interdimensional travel can be emotionally and mentally taxing. Prepare yourself mentally and emotionally for the experience by practicing mindfulness and developing a support system.

Protection: Consider using protection techniques, such as creating a protective energy shield around yourself, to protect yourself from negative entities and energies.

Telekinesis can be a powerful tool for interdimensional travel. By manipulating energy fields, we can move between dimensions and explore new realities. However, interdimensional travel can be dangerous and it is important to approach it with caution. By researching, preparing mentally and emotionally, and using protection techniques, we can safely explore new dimensions and expand our understanding of the universe.

Chapter 18: Telekinetic Techniques for Communication with Spirits

Have you ever wanted to communicate with a loved one who has passed away, or with a spirit guide who can provide guidance and support? While some may be skeptical of the idea of communicating with spirits, there are those who believe that it is possible through the use of telekinesis.

In this chapter, we will explore how telekinesis can be used for communication with spirits, techniques for contacting spirits, and how to protect yourself during spirit communication.

Using Telekinesis for Communication with Spirits

Telekinesis can be used for communication with spirits by allowing us to tap into the energy fields that spirits exist within. By manipulating these energy fields, we can send and receive messages from spirits.

To use telekinesis for communication with spirits, follow these steps:

Focus your energy: The first step in communicating with spirits is to focus your energy. Take some time to relax and clear your mind. Focus your energy on the intention of communicating with spirits.

Connect with the energy field: Once you have focused your energy, imagine that you are connecting with the energy field that spirits exist within. Imagine that you are reaching out to them and that they are reaching back to you.

Send and receive messages: Once you have established a connection with the energy field, you can begin to send and receive messages. Focus your energy on the message you want to send, and visualize it traveling through the energy field. Pay attention to any messages or images that come to you in response.

Techniques for Contacting Spirits

There are many techniques that can be used for contacting spirits, and the most effective technique will depend on the individual. Here are some techniques that may be helpful:

Meditation: Meditation is a powerful tool that can help you to focus your energy and connect with the energy fields that spirits exist within. By meditating regularly, you may be able to develop your telekinetic abilities and improve your ability to communicate with spirits.

Automatic writing: Automatic writing is the ability to write without consciously thinking about what you are writing. By practicing automatic writing, you may be able to receive messages from spirits.

To use automatic writing, focus your energy on the intention of communicating with spirits. Hold a pen and paper, and let your hand move freely. Pay attention to the words that come to you.

Pendulum dowsing: Pendulum dowsing is the use of a weighted object, such as a crystal or pendant, to communicate with spirits. By asking yes or no questions and observing the movement of the pendulum, you may be able to receive messages from spirits.

To use pendulum dowsing, hold the weighted object and ask a yes or no question. Observe the movement of the pendulum in response.

How to Protect Yourself During Spirit Communication

While communicating with spirits can be a rewarding and enlightening experience, it is important to protect yourself from any negative energies that may be present. Here are some tips for protecting yourself during spirit communication:

Set intentions: Before communicating with spirits, set clear intentions for what you want to achieve. Focus your energy on positive and uplifting intentions.

Use protection techniques: There are many protection techniques that can be used during spirit communication, such as visualizing a shield of white light around you, or asking for the protection of your spirit guides.

Trust your intuition: Pay attention to your intuition during spirit communication. If you feel uncomfortable or uneasy, trust your instincts and end the communication.

Ground yourself: Grounding techniques can help you to stay centered and balanced during spirit communication. To ground yourself, focus your energy on the earth, and imagine roots extending from your feet and into the ground.

Telekinesis is a powerful tool for communication with spirits, and can be used in conjunction with other techniques to facilitate spirit communication. However, it is important to approach spirit communication with respect and caution, and to protect yourself from any negative energies that may be present.

By setting clear intentions, using protection techniques, trusting your intuition, and grounding yourself, you can have a safe and positive experience when communicating with spirits. Remember to approach spirit communication with an open mind, and to be patient and persistent in your efforts.

Ultimately, the ability to communicate with spirits is a gift that can provide guidance and support, and can help us to connect with the spiritual world in a meaningful way. Whether you are communicating with a loved one who has passed away, or seeking guidance from a spirit guide, telekinesis can be a powerful tool in your spiritual journey.

Chapter 19: Telekinetic Techniques for Remote Viewing

Have you ever wanted to see a location that is far away or out of reach? Maybe you've dreamed of visiting a place you've never been to, or you're curious about what's happening in a different part of the world. With the power of telekinesis, it is possible to remotely view locations without physically being there.

In this chapter, we will explore how telekinesis can be used for remote viewing, techniques for seeing distant locations, and how to verify your remote viewing experiences.

Using Telekinesis for Remote Viewing

Telekinesis can be used for remote viewing by allowing us to tap into the energy fields that exist around a particular location. By manipulating these energy fields, we can gain insight into what is happening at that location, even if we are physically far away.

To use telekinesis for remote viewing, follow these steps:

Focus your energy: The first step in remote viewing is to focus your energy. Take some time to relax and clear your mind. Focus your energy on the intention of seeing a distant location.

Connect with the energy field: Once you have focused your energy, imagine that you are connecting with the energy field around the location you want to view. Imagine that you are reaching out to it and that it is reaching back to you.

Observe what you see: Once you have established a connection with the energy field, observe what you see. Pay attention to any images or messages that come to you. It may be helpful to keep a journal to record your remote viewing experiences.

Techniques for Seeing Distant Locations

There are many techniques that can be used for remote viewing, and the most effective technique will depend on the individual. Here are some techniques that may be helpful:

Guided visualization: Guided visualization is a technique in which you are guided through a mental journey to a particular location. This can be done with the help of a teacher, guide, or recorded meditation. Once you have reached the location in your mind, you can observe what you see.

Object association: Object association is a technique in which you use an object associated with the location you want to view to help you make a connection. For example, if you want to view a specific building, you could hold a photograph or a piece of paper with the building's address on it. Focus your energy on the object and imagine that you are connecting with the energy field around the building.

Astral projection: Astral projection is the ability to leave your physical body and travel to different locations in your astral body. This is an advanced technique that requires practice and may not be suitable for everyone. To astral project, relax and focus your energy on leaving your physical body. Imagine that you are floating out of your body and traveling to the location you want to view.

How to Verify Your Remote Viewing Experiences

It is important to verify your remote viewing experiences to ensure that they are accurate and not simply the result of imagination or wishful thinking. Here are some tips for verifying your remote viewing experiences:

Compare your observations: If possible, compare your observations with the actual location. For example, if you viewed a building, visit the building and compare what you saw to what is actually there.

Record your observations: Record your remote viewing experiences in a journal or on tape. Review your recordings periodically and compare them to actual locations or events.

Work with a partner: Work with a partner who can also view the location. Compare your observations and see if they match.

Trust your intuition: Pay attention to your intuition during remote viewing. If something doesn't feel right, trust your instincts and question your observations.

Telekinesis is a powerful tool that can be used for many purposes, including remote viewing. With practice and dedication, anyone can develop their telekinetic abilities and use them to explore the world beyond their physical reach. Remote viewing can provide valuable insights and information, and can also be a fun and interesting practice.

Remember to always approach remote viewing with an open mind and a positive attitude. Don't get discouraged if you don't get immediate results or if your experiences are not always accurate. Like any skill, telekinesis and remote viewing take time and practice to develop.

It's also important to use your telekinetic abilities ethically and responsibly. Avoid using them to invade others' privacy or for personal gain. Always approach remote viewing with the intention of learning or gaining insight, and be respectful of the energy fields you are tapping into.

Overall, remote viewing with telekinesis is a fascinating and worthwhile pursuit that can provide a new perspective on the world around us. So go ahead, explore and discover the power of your own mind!

Chapter 20: Telekinetic Techniques for Precognition

Have you ever had a feeling about something that was going to happen in the future? Maybe you had a premonition about a particular event or felt a strong intuition that something was going to occur. With the power of telekinesis, it is possible to develop the ability to predict the future.

In this chapter, we will explore how telekinesis can be used for precognition, techniques for predicting the future, and the ethics of using precognition.

Using Telekinesis for Precognition

Telekinesis can be used for precognition by tapping into the energy fields that exist around us. By manipulating these energy fields, we can gain insight into future events and predict what is going to happen.

To use telekinesis for precognition, follow these steps:

Focus your energy: The first step in developing precognition is to focus your energy. Take some time to relax and clear your mind. Focus your energy on the intention of predicting a future event.

Connect with the energy field: Once you have focused your energy, imagine that you are connecting with the energy field around you. Imagine that you are reaching out to it and that it is reaching back to you.

Observe what you see: Once you have established a connection with the energy field, observe what you see. Pay attention to any images or messages that come to you. It may be helpful to keep a journal to record your precognitive experiences.

Techniques for Predicting the Future

There are many techniques that can be used for precognition, and the most effective technique will depend on the individual. Here are some techniques that may be helpful:

Dreams: Dreams are a common way to receive precognitive information. Before going to sleep, focus your energy on the intention of receiving information about a future event. Keep a journal next to your bed and write down any dreams you have that may be related to your intention.

Meditation: Meditation is a powerful tool for developing precognition. During meditation, focus your energy on the intention of receiving information about a future event. Observe any images or messages that come to you.

Divination tools: Divination tools, such as tarot cards or runes, can be used to receive precognitive information. Focus your energy on the intention of receiving information about a future event, and then use the divination tool to interpret the messages.

The Ethics of Using Precognition

While precognition can be a powerful tool for gaining insight into future events, it is important to consider the ethical implications of using this ability. Here are some ethical considerations to keep in mind:

Free will: It is important to respect the free will of others. Predicting the future may give you insight into what is going to happen, but it is important to remember that individuals have the right to make their own choices.

Misuse of information: If you do receive information about a future event, it is important to use this information ethically. Using this information for personal gain or to harm others is unethical.

False predictions: It is important to remember that not all predictions will come true. False predictions can cause unnecessary fear or anxiety and can be harmful to others.

Telekinesis can be used for precognition, allowing us to gain insight into future events. While this ability can be a powerful tool, it is important to use it ethically and to respect the free will of others. With practice and dedication, anyone can develop their telekinetic abilities and use them to gain insight into the future.

Chapter 21: Telekinetic Techniques for Retrocognition

Have you ever wished you could go back in time and witness a historical event, or learn more about your family's past? With the power of telekinesis, you can tap into the energy fields that exist around past events and gain insight into what happened.

In this chapter, we will explore how telekinesis can be used for retrocognition, techniques for seeing the past, and how to interpret retrocognitive experiences.

Using Telekinesis for Retrocognition

Telekinesis can be used for retrocognition by allowing us to access the energy fields that exist around past events. By manipulating these energy fields, we can gain insight into what happened and even witness events that have already occurred.

To use telekinesis for retrocognition, follow these steps:

Focus your energy: The first step in retrocognition is to focus your energy. Take some time to relax and clear your mind. Focus your energy on the intention of seeing a past event.

Connect with the energy field: Once you have focused your energy, imagine that you are connecting with the energy field around the past event. Imagine that you are reaching out to it and that it is reaching back to you.

Observe what you see: Once you have established a connection with the energy field, observe what you see. Pay attention to any images or messages that come to you. It may be helpful to keep a journal to record your retrocognitive experiences.

Techniques for Seeing the Past

There are many techniques that can be used for retrocognition, and the most effective technique will depend on the individual. Here are some techniques that may be helpful:

Object association: Object association is a technique in which you use an object associated with the past event to help you make a connection. For example, if you want to view a specific historical event, you could hold a photograph or a replica of an object from that time period. Focus your energy on the object and imagine that you are connecting with the energy field around the event.

Guided visualization: Guided visualization is a technique in which you are guided through a mental journey to a particular time and place. This can be done with the help of a teacher, guide, or recorded meditation. Once you have reached the past event in your mind, you can observe what you see.

Dreams: Dreams can be a powerful tool for retrocognition. Before going to bed, focus your energy on the past event you want to view. Keep a dream journal by your bed and record any dreams or visions you have related to the past event.

How to Interpret Retrocognitive Experiences

Interpreting retrocognitive experiences can be challenging, as the images and messages that come through may not always be clear or easy to understand. Here are some tips for interpreting retrocognitive experiences:

Trust your intuition: Pay attention to your intuition during retrocognition. If something doesn't feel right, trust your instincts and question your observations.

Compare your observations: If possible, compare your observations with historical records or other sources of information about the past event. This can help you validate your experiences and gain a better understanding of what happened.

Keep a journal: Record your retrocognitive experiences in a journal. Write down any images or messages you receive, as well as any emotions or physical sensations you experience. Over time, you may start to notice patterns or themes that can help you interpret your experiences.

The Ethics of Using Retrocognition

As with any form of telekinesis, it is important to consider the ethics of using retrocognition. Here are some ethical considerations to keep in mind:

Respect the privacy of others: When using retrocognition to view past events involving other people, it is important to respect their privacy. Avoid using retrocognition to invade someone's personal space or violate their privacy.

Use retrocognition for positive purposes: It is important to use retrocognition for positive purposes and to avoid using it to harm others or interfere with their lives.

Obtain consent: If you plan to use retrocognition to view a past event involving another person, it is important to obtain their consent. This can be done through communication, either verbally or through telepathy.

Do not become overly reliant on retrocognition: It is important to remember that retrocognition is just one tool for gaining insight into the past. It is important to also rely on other sources of information, such as historical records and personal accounts.

Telekinesis can be a powerful tool for gaining insight into the past through retrocognition. By accessing the energy fields that exist around past events, we can gain valuable information and even witness events that have already occurred. However, it is important to use retrocognition ethically and for positive purposes. With practice and patience, anyone can develop their telekinetic abilities and explore the mysteries of the past.

Chapter 22: Telekinetic Techniques for Psychokinesis

Have you ever wanted to communicate with someone without speaking a single word? With telepathy, you can do just that. Telepathy is the ability to communicate with others using only the power of your mind. In this chapter, we will explore how telekinesis can be used for telepathy, techniques for sending and receiving messages telepathically, and the potential benefits and drawbacks of telepathy.

Using Telekinesis for Telepathy

Telekinesis can be used for telepathy by allowing you to access the energy fields that exist around the minds of other people. By manipulating these energy fields, you can communicate with others using only your thoughts.

To use telekinesis for telepathy, follow these steps:

Focus your energy: The first step in telepathy is to focus your energy. Take some time to relax and clear your mind. Focus your energy on the intention of sending or receiving a message telepathically.

Connect with the energy field: Once you have focused your energy, imagine that you are connecting with the energy field around the mind of the person you want to communicate with. Imagine that you are reaching out to it and that it is reaching back to you.

Send or receive your message: Once you have established a connection with the energy field, you can send or receive your message. To send a message, simply think about what you want to communicate. To receive a message, pay attention to any thoughts or images that come to you.

Techniques for Sending and Receiving Messages Telepathically

There are many techniques that can be used for telepathy, and the most effective technique will depend on the individual. Here are some techniques that may be helpful:

Visualizations: Visualization techniques can be used to send or receive telepathic messages. For example, you can visualize a beam of light connecting your mind with the mind of the person you want to communicate with.

Meditation: Meditation can be used to quiet the mind and enhance your telepathic abilities. By meditating regularly, you can develop your ability to focus your energy and connect with the energy fields around the minds of others.

Symbolic communication: Symbolic communication involves using symbols to communicate telepathically. For example, you can visualize a heart to express love or a question mark to ask a question.

The Potential Benefits and Drawbacks of Telepathy

Telepathy can be a powerful tool for communication, but it also has its drawbacks. Here are some potential benefits and drawbacks of telepathy:

Benefits:

Enhanced communication: Telepathy allows for communication without the need for spoken language, which can be beneficial for individuals who are deaf or mute.

Improved relationships: Telepathy can improve relationships by allowing for a deeper level of understanding between individuals.

Improved empathy: Telepathy can improve empathy by allowing individuals to connect with the thoughts and feelings of others.

Drawbacks:

Privacy concerns: Telepathy raises concerns about privacy, as it could potentially allow for the invasion of an individual's thoughts and feelings without their consent.

Mental overload: Telepathy could potentially lead to mental overload, as individuals may be bombarded with thoughts and feelings from others.

Misinterpretation of messages: Telepathic messages can be easily misinterpreted, as individuals may not be able to fully understand the context or intention behind a message.

Telepathy is a fascinating and powerful ability that can be developed using telekinesis. With the right techniques and practice, anyone can learn to communicate telepathically. However, it is important to consider the potential benefits and drawbacks of telepathy before attempting to use this ability. By using telepathy responsibly and with respect for others, we can unlock a new level of communication and understanding.

Chapter 23: Troubleshooting Telekinetic Blocks

Telekinesis can be a challenging skill to master, and it is not uncommon to encounter obstacles along the way. In this chapter, we will discuss common obstacles to telekinetic progress, strategies for overcoming telekinetic blocks, and ways to deal with frustration and self-doubt.

Identifying Common Obstacles to Telekinetic Progress

There are several common obstacles that people may encounter when trying to develop their telekinetic abilities. These include:

Lack of focus: One of the most common obstacles to telekinetic progress is a lack of focus. Telekinesis requires a high level of concentration, and distractions can easily disrupt your focus and prevent you from making progress.

Negative beliefs: Negative beliefs about your own abilities can also hinder your progress. If you believe that you are not capable of developing telekinetic abilities, you may inadvertently create self-imposed limits that prevent you from making progress.

Stress and anxiety: Stress and anxiety can also make it difficult to develop telekinetic abilities. These emotions can interfere with your ability to focus and make it harder to connect with the energy necessary for telekinesis.

Lack of practice: Like any skill, telekinesis requires regular practice. If you are not practicing regularly, it can be difficult to make progress and develop your abilities.

Strategies for Overcoming Telekinetic Blocks

If you are encountering obstacles in your telekinetic practice, there are several strategies that you can use to overcome them. These include:

Meditation: Meditation can be a powerful tool for improving focus and reducing stress and anxiety. Regular meditation can help you to develop the mental clarity necessary for telekinesis.

Affirmations: Affirmations are positive statements that can help to shift negative beliefs and self-imposed limits. By repeating positive affirmations about your abilities, you can create a more positive mindset and increase your confidence.

Visualization: Visualization is the process of creating a mental image of what you want to achieve. By visualizing yourself successfully performing telekinetic feats, you can increase your belief in your own abilities and help to overcome self-doubt.

Regular practice: Regular practice is essential for developing telekinetic abilities. By practicing regularly, you can improve your focus and develop the muscle memory necessary for telekinesis.

Dealing with Frustration and Self-Doubt

Even with regular practice and a positive mindset, it is not uncommon to experience frustration and self-doubt when developing telekinetic abilities. Here are some strategies for dealing with these emotions:

Take a break: If you are feeling frustrated or overwhelmed, it may be helpful to take a break from practicing. Give yourself time to recharge and come back to your practice with renewed focus and energy.

Celebrate small successes: When you experience small successes in your telekinetic practice, take the time to celebrate them. Celebrating your successes can help to build your confidence and motivate you to continue practicing.

Seek support: Joining a community of like-minded individuals who are also working on developing their telekinetic abilities can be a great source of support and motivation. Consider joining a telekinesis group or forum to connect with others and share your experiences.

Developing telekinetic abilities requires patience, practice, and a positive mindset. While there may be obstacles and challenges along the way, with dedication and persistence, you can achieve your telekinetic goals. Remember to focus on the process and celebrate your successes, no matter how small they may seem. With time and practice, you can tap into the power of telekinesis and unlock your full potential.

Chapter 24: Continuing Your Telekinetic Journey

Congratulations on reaching the end of this book on telekinesis! By now, you have learned about the basics of telekinesis, various techniques to improve your skills, and how to overcome obstacles along the way.

However, your journey with telekinesis doesn't have to end here. There are plenty of resources available for you to continue your exploration and learning. Here are some suggestions:

Online resources: The internet is a treasure trove of information on telekinesis. You can find forums, online communities, YouTube channels, and websites dedicated to telekinesis. However, make sure to be discerning with the information you consume and always check the sources.

Books: There are many books available on telekinesis, both in physical and electronic form. Some recommended titles are "The Telekinesis Handbook: Developing Your Powers" by Dr. James Harte and "Telekinesis for Beginners: The Ultimate Guide to Moving Objects and Unleashing the Full Potential of Your Mind" by David Petry.

Workshops and classes: Consider attending workshops or classes on telekinesis if they are available in your area. It can be a great way to meet others interested in telekinesis and learn from experienced teachers.

Creating a telekinetic community and support system can also be beneficial for your journey. Joining a group or creating one yourself can provide a space to share experiences, exchange tips and techniques, and support each other.

As you continue your telekinetic journey, it's essential to set goals for continued progress and growth. Having clear goals can help you stay motivated and focused. Start by setting small, achievable goals, and gradually work your way up to bigger ones.

Lastly, remember that frustration and self-doubt are natural and common experiences when developing telekinetic abilities. Be patient with yourself and celebrate your progress, no matter how small. Practicing regularly and consistently is the key to success.

Thank you for reading this book on telekinesis. I hope that it has provided you with useful information and techniques to help you on your telekinetic journey. Remember to stay curious, stay motivated, and most importantly, have fun!

Don't miss out!

Visit the website below and you can sign up to receive emails whenever SERGIO RIJO publishes a new book. There's no charge and no obligation.

https://books2read.com/r/B-A-COYW-XBBIC

BOOKS 2 READ

Connecting independent readers to independent writers.

Also by SERGIO RIJO

Anime Tattoo Design Book: 300+ Designs for Fans and Tattoo Artists

The Art of Butterfly Tattoos: 300+ Designs to Inspire Your Next Tattoo

Rose Tattoo Designs: 300+ Designs to Inspire Your Next Tattoo

The Geometric Tattoo Handbook: A Complete Collection of 300+ Designs

Skull Tatoo Designs: Over 300 Tattoo Designs to Inspire You

Soulful: Unlocking the 16 Traits of Advanced Souls

Memory Mastery: The Proven System to Retain Information Effectively

Rise and Shine: A Guide to Kundalini Awakening for the Modern Spiritual Seeker

The Power of Presence: Connecting with Your Higher Self and Living with Purpose

Powerful Techniques for Mastering the Art of Influence: Proven Strategies to Exert Maximum Power and Persuasion

The Art of Remote Viewing: A Step-by-Step Guide to Unlocking Your Psychic Abilities

Money Magnetism: The Art of Attracting Abundance

The Happiness Handbook: A Practical Guide to Finding Joy and Fulfillment

The Smarter You: Proven Ways to Boost Your Intelligence

Appetite Control Strategies: The Secret to Successful Weight Loss

Off The Grid Living: A Comprehensive Guide to Sustainable and Self-Sufficient Living

The Ultimate Guide to Get Your Ex Back: A Step-by-Step Blueprint to Rekindle Love and Heal Your Relationship

Calm and Centered: Overcoming Anxiety and Panic Attacks Naturally

The Power Within: Boosting Self-Esteem and Confidence through Positive Self-Talk and Self-Care Practices

Grateful Living: Transform Your Life with the Power of Gratitude

Procrastination Uncovered: Understanding and Overcoming the Epidemic of Delay

Social Butterfly: Tips and Strategies for Conquering Shyness and Social Anxiety

Living with Purpose: Finding Meaning and Direction in Life":

Breaking Free from Self-Sabotage: Overcoming Destructive Patterns and Achieving Your Goals

Uncovering the Shadows: A Journey through Shadow Work

The Science of Nutrition for Athletes: Understanding the Specific Nutritional Needs of Athletes for Optimal Performance and Recovery

The Magic of Saying No: How to Establish Boundaries and Take Charge of Your Life

Connecting with the Divine: Tools and Techniques for Powerful Prayer

Living in Harmony: The Complete Guide to Permaculture and Sustainable Living

Angelic Assistance: How to Connect with Your Guardian Angels and Spirit Guides for Support

Beyond Belief: Unraveling the Psychology of Ghosts and Hauntings

Transform Your Health with Intermittent Fasting: A Comprehensive Guide to Techniques and Benefits

Discover the Secrets of Lucid Dreaming: How to Use Your Dreams to Transform Your Life

Existential Crisis: Strategies for Finding Hope and Renewal in Life's Darkest Moments

The 12 Spiritual Laws of the Universe: A Comprehensive Guide to Achieving Personal Growth and Spiritual Enlightenment

The 144,000 Lightworkers: Healing and Awakening Humanity to Save the World

Defying Age: The Ultimate Guide to Living a Long and Healthy Life

Unlocking the Secrets of Astral Projection: Techniques for Successful Out-of-Body Experiences

Inner Child Healing: The Key to Overcoming Negative Beliefs, Self-Sabotage, and Unlocking Your True Potential

Raising Your Vibration: A Holistic Guide to Achieving Emotional and Spiritual Well-being

Psychic Vampires and Empaths: The Ultimate Guide to Protection and Healing with Energy, Crystals, Reiki, and More

Developing Clairvoyance: The Ultimate Guide to Unlocking Your Psychic Gifts and Connecting with the Spiritual World

Mastering Telekinesis: A Step-by-Step Guide to Developing Your Psychokinetic Abilities

About the Author

Join me on an adventure through captivating stories! I'm Sergio Rijo, a passionate writer with 20 years of experience in crafting books across genres. Let's explore new worlds together and get hooked from start to finish.

Milton Keynes UK
Ingram Content Group UK Ltd.
UKHW021039190124
436321UK00001BA/9